Brutalist Interiors

Blue Crow Media

Brut
Inte

alist

iors

With essays by Blake Gopnik, Ewan Harrison, Deane Madsen, Gili Merin, Naomi Pollock, Ljubica Slavković, Felix Torkar and Rixt Woudstra

Blue Crow Media
London, United Kingdom
bluecrowmedia.com

First published 2025

ISBN 978-1-912018-22-2

A CIP Catalogue record for this book
is available from the British Library.

Edited and published by Derek Lamberton
Copy edited by Hattie Crisell
Designed by Tuomi
Printed by Verona Libri
Published by Blue Crow Media

This book and other titles are available
to purchase from bluecrowmedia.com.

Front cover: Housden House © Taran Wilkhu

Foreword

Growing up in Washington, DC inclines a person towards Brutalist and concrete interiors. Foremost in my memory of a happy childhood spent there are weekend outings via the sombre platforms and endless escalators of Harry Weese's Metro, to the bright concrete ceilings and marvellous bridges of IM Pei's East Building of the National Gallery. This convergence of Brutalism and Modernism, while visually beyond the brick and shingles of my weekday Washington, is as essential to it in my memory as the summer sun on the city's sidewalks and the branches of its trees.

This book follows a decade of publishing guides to Brutalist and concrete architecture around the world. The joy of this work has been meeting many of the guides' authors and photographers (some of whom have contributed to this publication) in their cities, and visiting the featured buildings alongside this book's designer, Jaakko Tuomivaara. Over this period, I've seen countless Brutalist buildings demolished, left in states of irrecoverable neglect, obscured by multi-storey advertisements or even masked behind crooked Neoclassical façades. In many cases, the sense of architecture becoming sediment is all too real. However, I have also observed Brutalist buildings thriving as part of people's daily lives. The rarest of these examples include buildings with nearly unaltered interiors, such as Belgrade's Sava Centre as described in Ljubica Slavković's essay. The thrill of stepping inside a complex building like this is what I hope to convey with this book.

The photographers featured here have transported and inspired countless people with their work, and have been critical to our understanding and to the rising popularity of Brutalism. The selection of photographs chosen for this book seeks to place the movement within its international context while emphasising variety and highlighting lesser known interiors.

The essays that follow are by writers whose work has educated us as to what architects have done and continue to do with concrete. It should be mentioned that not every architect whose work is featured here considers it to be Brutalist, and not every building presented is necessarily so. But all meet the broad definition of Brutalism, or, as Felix Torkar describes in his essay on Neobrutalism, have become part of the movement's story as it forges into the future.

However counterintuitive it may be to some of us, an understanding of Brutalist buildings as houses of worship, with connections to our deepest traditions, is covered in Gili Merin's essay about Vienna's Wotruba Church. The essay by Rixt Woudstra and Ewan Harrison describes, amongst other things, the subtle continuity between the exterior and interior of a pair of buildings in Ghana. The resonance of history and blurred lines are also explored in Naomi Pollock's writing about the interiors of Tadao Ando. Weese's aforementioned Washington Metro is thoroughly examined by Deane Madsen, providing not only a personal starting point for my fellow Washingtonians (some of whom remain notably unconvinced), but an insight into the complexities of designing within a bureaucracy, as so many architects of Brutalist buildings were.

Finally, it is Blake Gopnik's essay about growing up in Habitat 67 that might provide the reader with a eureka moment, as he reflects on how the building blocks of his aesthetic taste formed inside the (concrete, needless to say) building blocks of his childhood home.

Derek Lamberton
London, 2025

Cafeteria, Caracas University City

Carlos Raúl Villanueva, 1953
Caracas, Venezuela

Chacarita Cemetery
Itala Fulvia Villa, Clorindo Testa, 1950–58
Buenos Aires, Argentina

Saint John's Abbey Church

Marcel Breuer, 1961
Collegeville, MN, USA

Palace of Assembly

Le Corbusier, 1951–62
Chandigarh, India

Sheats-Goldstein Residence

John Lautner, 1963

Los Angeles, CA, USA

Butantã Houses

Paulo Mendes da Rocha, 1964
São Paulo, Brazil

Piraque Industrial Complex

Marcello Fragelli, 1964

Rio de Janeiro, Brazil

Andrée Bordeaux-Le Pecq House

Claude Parent, 1963–65

Bois-le-Roy, France

Temple of Monte Grisa

Antonio Guacci, Sergio Musmeci, 1965
Trieste, Italy

Inside-Outside: Brutalist Interiors in West Africa

Rixt Woudstra and Ewan Harrison

In the late 1950s and '60s, as many West African countries became independent, a variety of Brutalist buildings emerged across the region, including schools, universities, museums, libraries, banks and offices. These strikingly Modern buildings embodied the optimism of newly independent nations like Ghana.

Contrary to Brutalist buildings in Europe or North America, however, many of these structures were designed to open up to the exterior, creating a fluid boundary between inside and outside. West Africa's tropical climate pushed architects—who were often still European, even after independence—to rethink the relationship between the interior and exterior. Rather than creating a sealed-off envelope, they used techniques that stimulated the flow of air while preventing the sun from entering. The façade was a key technology to this process of modulation. Architects deployed a consistent design vocabulary of *brise soleil*, concrete screens and cantilevered canopies. The buildings consisted mostly of raw concrete, while other materials used, such as local tropical timber, marble or travertine created interesting visual effects.

Commercial Bank of Ghana, Takoradi, 1958

Better known for iconic Brutalist designs like London's National Theatre building (1976), British architect Denys Lasdun was also responsible for several projects in Ghana in the late 1950s, including the Commercial Bank of Ghana, today left vacant. Lasdun completed the striking travertine-clad concrete building in 1958. Located in the centre of Takoradi, one of the country's major port cities, it occupies a central spot on a main thoroughfare. The project's client was the Ghana Commercial Bank (GCB), a state-owned bank for Ghanaian traders and farmers, in partnership with the Bank of Ghana Currency Board, the

central bank's *bureau de change*. No expense was spared in this significant project for important clients—something reflected in the building's luxurious and mostly imported material palette, both outside and inside.

With a rubble-clad plinth, a protruding canopy over the entrance and a strongly expressed, overhanging roofline, the building exudes a sense of classicism. Sadly, many interior details have not survived. The imposing outer wall of travertine fins once concealed an inner wall of tinted glazing hung on horizontal pivots. This allowed for a breeze and the partial exclusion of sun penetration from the interior. The bank's internal space consisted of a double-height hall, with a manager's suite on one side and a mezzanine level of offices above. Both had internal façades facing into the banking hall composed of glass and dark local timber, a material that was also used in the counters and cashiers' desks distributed across the floor.

In the opposite rear corner, a cubic volume extended into the space of the banking hall, housing currency vaults. This was entirely clad in a deep green and blue marble, forming an enigmatic extrusion into the space, its upper level entered by a daringly cantilevered spiral staircase. This same dark marble was used to clad supporting piers throughout the interior.

While the control of sunlight into an interior space was a thermal requirement, Lasdun played with the visual experience of light, too. There is a deliberate contrast between light and darkness, with the golden travertine and white concrete of the façade belonging to the dazzling world of the exterior, whereas inside, the tinted glass, dark marble and timber created an atmosphere of tempered darkness.

Great Hall, Kwame Nkrumah University of Science and Technology, 1964–67

Built several years later, in a different part of Ghana, the Great Hall—still in use today—was designed as the centrepiece of the Kwame Nkrumah University of Science and Technology's campus in Kumasi. Standing on elevated ground, the two-storey building, with its striking concrete slab façade and overhanging roof, towers over the sprawling, tropical campus. While the campus was developed in the early 1950s under late-colonial British rule, the Great Hall was built after independence, between 1964 and 1967. Designed by the relatively unknown British architectural firm Gerlach and Gillies-Reyburn, the building consists of a 1600-seat auditorium for graduation ceremonies and other official events. Like Lasdun's Commercial Bank, the façade is partially open, consisting of precast concrete louvers to keep out the sun.

In addition to concrete, which dominates the exterior, Gerlach and Gillies-Reyburn used dark, gleaming tropical timber details in the interior spaces, particularly

the entrance section. Left open to the outside, this space is dotted with squared pilotis supporting the upper-level entrances to the auditorium. Especially striking are the deep-brown balustrades of the double staircase, set in the centre, made of local wood. (Sapele, located close to the Ivory Coast border, provided tropical timber to the domestic as well as British market in the 1950s and '60s). Alongside colourful murals depicting Ghanaian scenes—painted by students—the timber provides a warm, polished shine to the roughly textured grey concrete.

The two examples discussed here underline how architects reconsidered Brutalist designs in West Africa as permeable structures with fluid boundaries between the interior and exterior. As a result, the interior is often not considered a separate space; it is an extension, rather, of the outside—or a way of bringing the outside in.

Basilica-Cathedral of Our Lady of Altagracia

André Dunoyer de Segonzac, Pierre Dupré, 1949–71
Higüey, Dominican Republic

Housden House

Brian Housden, 1963–65
London, United Kingdom

Salk Institute

Louis Kahn, 1965
San Diego, CA, USA

Breuer Building
Marcel Breuer, 1966
New York, NY, USA

SALIDA

Former Bank of London

C Testa, SS Elía, FP Ramos, A Agostini, 1960–66
Buenos Aires, Argentina

Peel Métro Station

Papineau, Gérin-Lajoie, Le Blanc, 1966
Montréal, QC, Canada

RALLIEZ-VOUS
À LA RECHERCHE

Kerselare Chapel

Juliaan Lampens, 1961–66
Oudenaarde, Belgium

Saint Agnes Church (now König Gallery)

Werner Düttmann, 1965–67
Berlin, Germany

CEPT University, School of Architecture

Balkrishna Doshi, 1966–68
Ahmedabad, India

Johannes XXIII Church

Heinz Buchmann and Josef Rikus, 1968
Cologne, Germany

Church of Saint Paul

Fritz Schaller, 1966–68
Neuss, Germany

Growing Up in Habitat 67

Blake Gopnik

My fond memories of growing up atop Moshe Safdie's Habitat 67, a Montreal landmark that's almost certainly Canada's greatest building, include pain in my leg, felt at least once a month for much of my childhood.

The stairs in Habitat's apartments were built without risers, as just a series of treads held at their two ends; run up them too fast, as my five siblings and I often did, and you were likely to let a foot slip between treads, with a devastating effect on your shins.

Many people might see this as a design defect: style pursued at the expense of function (and bodily integrity). I can't say I enjoyed the shock and pain. But I now see those stairs as standing for Habitat's glories. Almost every moment spent there kept you awake to what it was, how it worked and how you (and your shins) felt about it.

That has always been most obvious when it comes to Habitat's exterior: its 354 modular almost-cubes, poured from concrete then stacked at odd angles like some giant's toy blocks, guarantee all kinds of sensory and cognitive jolts. Gaps between units invite you to squeeze through the space between them; cantilevers leave you fearing a sudden fall off an edge; concrete overhangs threaten from above.

Habitat's jungle-gym wonders and pleasures should hardly surprise, given an architect who was only twenty-two and still studying at McGill University when he came up with the concept. The country that brought the project to life was almost equally youthful: Habitat was a 100th-birthday present that Canada gave itself, as a housing pavilion at the Expo 67 world's fair in Montreal. That was a city also reveling in a new, youthful spirit, as its French Canadian majority escaped the shadow of its Catholic clergy and Anglo bosses, and made itself known on the world stage.

My parents, barely in their thirties, came to love the building and its city on a visit from Philadelphia in the summer of 1967, all six kids in tow. The eight of us moved

to Montreal the following year partly for the chance to live in Habitat, then offering rentals as a "normal" apartment building.

After some time crammed into a too-small unit just above ground level, we moved up into the only apartment truly big enough to hold us in some kind of comfort, assembled from four modules at the very top of the structure, spanning its tenth and eleventh floors. Inside our apartment, the more demonstrative surprises of the building's exterior were translated into domestic terms that were no less caffeinating.

The living room soared up, two stories tall, with overhangs and niches that recalled the cubist effects of the building's outside, keeping Habitat's structural principles always top of mind. Up one side of the room ran the apartment's perilous staircase, animating or even threatening the space beneath it. (You could see and hear and almost feel the feet of people going up and down; cleaning the treads one day, my father let our vacuum's nozzle fall through the crack between them, smashing one of my mother's attempts at neon sculpture on the floor below.)

At the top of the stairs, a narrow mezzanine ran the width of the room, like the choir loft in a church. For our family, at least, the effect was social as much as spatial: while the grownups enjoyed their fancy times out in the open in the living room below, we would peer down at them from the more intimate sanctuary of the mezzanine, cracking wise from our peanut gallery.

Because we expect domestic space to be so much more reserved, more sheltering, than our homes' public-facing exteriors, the subtlest gestures of Safdie's interiors could read as emphatic. Almost every detail of our apartment kept you aware of the special nature of its design, as though deconstructing it for a thesis (which Safdie actually had).

Safdie specced light switches that were just a white button, for on, and a black one, for off, thereby depicting their effects in their design. Habitat's bathrooms were likewise thematising. Custom-cast from white fibreglass in one monocoque piece, they functioned as illustrations of a post-war ideal of seamless hygiene, even as they offered up its outcomes. Just walking into one of our bathrooms, you could almost feel the smooth flow of Handi-Wipes across its sleek surfaces and the effect of Fantastik spray on its germs. (My family arrived in Montreal already addicted to both those brand-new cleaning products; we were shocked that our Canadian friends did not know them.)

In our apartment, all windows came down to within three or four inches of the floor—not such a radical move at first sight, but it encouraged fears and fantasies of tumbling through the glass and out into empty space beyond. One tight corner of the living room was entirely walled in glass; the parquet before it stayed notably empty during even the most crowded New Year's Eve parties. (Up in our peanut gallery, we kids laughed at the guests' trepidation.)

On our top floor, beyond the mezzanine, a narrow hallway connecting our bedrooms was windowed the entire length of one side, offering a view out onto a vertical drop down eleven stories; I remember an otherwise rambunctious school friend who absolutely refused to walk the hallway's length.

After only a half-decade, we Gopniks abandoned Habitat to spend a year and more criss-crossing Europe in a Citroën station wagon—a DS, "The Goddess" hymned by Roland Barthes—and Safdie himself took over our apartment. In 2022, he donated it to McGill, and it's now restored to its 1967 state and open for tours. On a return visit, I was amazed at how many of my original impressions of the apartment had remained intact. Everything about it still made me wake up and take notice. (I walked up those stairs with overlearned care.)

In his recent writings on aesthetics, the Berkeley philosopher Alva Noë has drawn a distinction between the "tools" we encounter unthinkingly as we go about our daily lives—wedding dances, photos in advertisements and, of relevance to this essay, standard homes—and the "strange tools" that may look and feel much the same, but in fact function as that other thing sometimes called "art". The strange tools of art include the objects in our museums, the choreographies on our stages and certain special structures, such as Habitat, that are more "architecture" than merely "construction". The point Noe makes is that when a human creation gets us to ponder the kind of thing it is, and what we might want to do with and to it, at that very moment—and possibly only for that one short moment in its otherwise pedestrian life—it rises to a different cultural level, with new functions that might count as positively philosophical.

Habitat offered more such moments, daily, than almost anywhere else you might live. It established an aesthetic standard that all other art has had to live up to, in my life since.

Tomie Ohtake Residence

Ruy Ohtake, 1968–70
São Paulo, Brazil

Atelier Rosa

Hermann Rosa, 1968
Munich, Germany

Ariosto Martirani House

João Batista Vilanova Artigas, 1969
São Paulo, Brazil

Resurrection of Christ Parish Church

Günther Domenig and Eilfried Huth, 1969

Oberwart, Austria

504
75
208 124
108

Holy Cross Church

Walter Maria Förderer, 1969
Chur, Switzerland

LEFT SIDE
TICKETS
7

Thorndike Theatre
(now Leatherhead Theatre)

Roderick Ham, 1969

Leatherhead, United Kingdom

Science & Engineering South
University of Illinois Chicago

Skidmore, Owings & Merrill (SOM), 1968
Chicago, IL, USA

BIOLOGY
&
ADVISING OFFICE
EXIT
TO PLAZA
EXIT

Ontario Science Centre

Moriyama & Teshima, 1969
Toronto, ON, Canada

The Sculpted Interiors of Wotruba Church

Gili Merin

It is rare for a church to bear the name of its architect; not even Gaudí, who shaped Barcelona's skyline with the Sagrada Familia, received such an honour. Yet in Vienna, a city where Baroque traditions blend with quirky Deconstructivism, it is to be expected that the Kirche Zur Heiligsten Dreifaltigkeit (Church of the Most Holy Trinity)—a stack of concrete monoliths overlooking the city—would be simply named after the sculptor who conceived it. The Wotrubakirche (Wotruba Church) was designed by Fritz Wotruba, an Austrian sculptor of Czech-Hungarian origin.

Born in 1907 and growing up in an abusive family, Wotruba found solace and purpose in stone engraving, drawing and sculpting, becoming a celebrated artist in the early 1930s. Having fled to Switzerland during the Nazi occupation, he returned to Austria in 1945 determined to revive the city's cultural landscape. As a professor of sculpture at the Academy of Fine Arts in Vienna, he spear-headed efforts to restore the artistic vibrancy of the city. It was during this period that he designed the enormous sculpture that would ultimately become the church—a creation that would achieve "perfect unity with the landscape, the architecture and the city".

The building of the Wotrubakirche was initiated by the Austrian economist Margarethe Ottillinger, as a response to what she perceived as society's growing secularisation. She envisaged the church as a modern beacon of Catholic faith, and fittingly chose a site on top of a wooded hill on the outskirts of Vienna, surrounded by forests and hiking trails. The spot had previously been home to a Nazi barrack, and Ottillinger was moved to transform a place of oppression, violence and racism into one of lightness, faith and hope.

Though the design was conceived before the location was selected, it appears tailored to its setting. It was architect Fritz Gerhard Mayer—often overlooked—who transformed Wotruba's sculpture into a functional church, built between 1974 and 1976. Wotruba died in 1975, before the project was completed.

It is as much an artwork as a building. It is conceived of no less than 152 concrete monoliths that weigh between 1.84 and 141 tonnes each. The blocks are stacked vertically and diagonally to form a structure that Wotruba claimed was inspired by the Gothic cathedral in Chartres—albeit a *béton brut* interpretation. This arrangement creates a porous sense of space between the interior and the exterior landscape through the use

of undecorated glass panels that allow an abundance of daylight. From a distance, the church arguably looks like a concrete version of Stonehenge, as no two blocks are alike, and their asymmetrical arrangement evokes prehistoric ritual and mysterious construction techniques.

Inside, a sense of archaic architecture also reverberates in the church's floor plan, which resembles a Neolithic shelter in its haphazard arrangement of loose stones around a central hearth—here represented by the faux-marble altar. While the main nave retains a classical elongated composition, its ritualistic focus is centralised, with seating arranged on both sides to encourage a shared, rather than the typical one-directional, orientation for sermons. There is additional seating in the protruding side chapel, which offers a more intimate space. This chapel has a lowered concrete ceiling that transitions into a bright annex, enveloped on three sides by the surrounding park. The asymmetrical floor plan creates a seemingly chaotic stacking of concrete blocks, which, according to Wotruba, achieves a "harmonic unity".

A bronze crucifix placed across from the main entrance gives a focal point to the nave. This faceless, geometrically jagged figure of Christ, originally designed by Wotruba for a church in Germany, was reproduced for the Wotrubakirche. It serves as a reminder of his primary occupation as a sculptor with a strong inclination toward figurative abstraction.

Wotruba's background as an object-maker, rather than an architect, is evident in certain construction details of the church. The ceiling, initially conceived as flat, now bears visible drainage stains, suggesting inadequate maintenance and design shortcomings. Considering the building was inspired by a Gothic cathedral, the incorporation of vaults, domes or other forms of vertical articulation might have introduced complexity to the interior that could have matched the striking character of the exterior.

Though the marriage between Brutalism and buildings of faith seems unlikely, Vienna boasts an array of concrete masterpieces (including some with impressive ceilings) that emerged during the Catholic construction boom of the post-war period. This includes the cubic Konzilsgedächtniskirche (Council Memorial Church) in Lainz-Speising by Josef Lackner from 1968. This church, devoid of windows, has a sky-lit ceiling that floods the interior—crafted of concrete, steel and mustard-coloured carpets—in soft, indirect natural light. A few kilometres away is the Oberbaumgarten Church by Johann Georg Gsteu from 1965. This modular rectangular building of reinforced concrete follows a centralised plan. Its ceiling—a structural waffled concrete punctured by a fenestrated cross—draws inspiration from the Pantheon's use of coffered concrete and natural light.

Other notable Brutalist churches in Vienna include the Pfarrkirche St Florian (1962), distinguished by its stained glass and diagonal concrete ribs, and the Evangelical Glaubenskirche in Simmering (1963) featuring a minimalist use of concrete, brick and glass, meant to evoke "the restrained and withdrawn" character of Protestant rituals, according to its architect, Roland Rainer.

These Brutalist churches, with the Wotrubakirche as their most iconic example, are vital to Vienna's diverse architectural landscape. They mark moments of austere aesthetics among the mesmerising Baroque and Jugendstil (a Viennese version of Art Nouveau) structures that predated them, as well as the radical Postmodernism and expressive Deconstructivism that followed. While these architectural movements did not originate in Vienna, they became deeply enmeshed in the city, where artistic experimentation is encouraged and celebrated with public commissions in central locations. From Fischer von Erlach through Otto Wagner and Adolf Loos to Hans Hollein and Hermann Czech, Fritz Wotruba joins an extraordinary lineage of visionary architects who not only shaped the architecture of the city, but also defined iconic movements that spread beyond the Austrian capital and even beyond Europe.

Additional photograph on page 123.

Cafeteria, Saarland University

Walter Schrempf and Otto Herbert Hajek, 1963–70
Saarbrücken, Germany

Saint Nicholas Church

Walter Maria Förderer, 1962–71
Hérémence, Switzerland

Burroughs Wellcome / Elion-Hitchings Building

Paul Rudolph, 1972
Research Triangle Park, NC, USA

CBR Building

Constantin Brodzki, Marcel Lambrichs, 1967–70
Brussels, Belgium

Hauts-de-Seine Prefecture

André Wogenscky, 1973

Nanterre, France

Cathedral of Saint Mary of the Assumption

Pier Luigi Nervi, Pietro Belluschi, 1971
San Francisco, CA, USA

49th Street Subway Station

Philip Johnson, John Burgee, 1973
New York, NY, USA

Clifton Cathedral

R Weeks, F Jennett, A Poremba, 1969–73
Renovation by Purcell, 2018
Bristol, United Kingdom

Robarts Library, University of Toronto

Warner, Burns, Toan & Lunde,
Mathers & Haldenby, 1973
Toronto, ON, Canada

The Sublime Beauty of Tadao Ando's Concrete

Naomi Pollock

The concrete interiors of Tadao Ando are as much an aesthetic experience as an architectural medium. His walls may be rock solid, but they are as smooth as a baby's bottom. They may appear cold and exposed, but they feel warm and protective. They may seem spare and unadorned, but close inspection reveals subtle variegations and patterning.

Certainly, Ando was not the first Japanese designer to elevate this once lowly, industrial material. Junzo Yoshimura sought its impenetrability for his own Mountain Cottage in Karuizawa. Kazuo Shinohara expressed its brawn inside the House in Uehara. And Takamitsu Azuma needed its plasticity to mold the tiny, triangular rooms of Tower House. But it was Ando who first recognised—and realised—the sublime beauty of an interior concrete wall well-crafted.

Ando is quick to explain that his use of concrete segued organically from Japan's own material palette. For centuries, readily available wood, paper, bamboo, *tatami* and rammed earth have been turned into architectural elements by skilled artisans up and down the archipelago. Some were finished with a sealant, but others were left to wear and weather—especially those inside. Only with the passage of time could patina develop, sharp edges smooth down and true beauty emerge. Applied ornament or decoration was largely limited to built-in furnishings like *tokonoma* display alcoves, staggered *chigaidana* shelves or painted *fusuma* sliding screens. But beauty was everywhere. Completely integrated with the building fabric, it was perceptible in woven bamboo ceilings, milky white *shoji* panels and *tatami* mat floors. Each element added colour, texture, exquisite detailing and, implicitly, the presence of the maker's hand.

For Ando those crafters are the tradespeople who build his architecture. "Close collaboration among various workers (formwork, rebar, concrete, electrical and mechanical) is essential," explains the architect. This is achieved in part once the project has gone on site and the designer's field office has been set up. The norm in Japan, this practice enables architects to communicate constantly with the contractors and weigh in on even the smallest of design or construction decisions as they crop up. Nowadays, machines may do the proverbial heavy lifting, but they have yet to supersede the critical input by the human hand and eye.

One of the keys to Ando's success comes from the construction of the concrete itself. Basically, all Ando walls, inside as well as out, are made of poured-in-place, reinforced concrete molded by wooden forms. "Formwork is one of the most important procedures in creating exposed concrete. The involvement of skilled carpenters is just as essential as it is in traditional Japanese architecture," explains Ando. Built with exactitude and precision, the forms consist of plywood panels coated with urethane resin, which contributes to the super smooth surface of Ando's concrete.

Another tie to history, each plywood panel measures 900×1800 mm—the same dimensions of the typical *tatami* mat. Proportional to the recumbent human body, the *tatami* mat dictated the measurements and placement of many architectural elements in traditional Japanese buildings. Even today it remains an important size reference for manufacturers, contractors and estate agents as well as the consumer.

Aside from exposed pinholes inside and waterproof sealant on the outside, there is little difference between Ando's interior and exterior walls. This underscores the ambiguous boundary that is a characteristic of many traditional buildings and a prevalent theme in Ando's architecture. In his House in Ginza, concrete walls and gridded pavers carry over from living areas to balconies.

The interior of the Kidosaki House opens onto a courtyard, itself an outdoor room rendered in concrete. And the House in Utsubo Park visually engages the greenery next door.

Even in the heart of the city, an Ando building connects directly to the environment—light, air, greenery and sky—which activates its interior. "We think that concrete is a natural material that works as a backdrop for daylight, art, furniture and other elements of daily life activities," explains the architect. As in the Koshino House, sliver-like skylights and carefully considered windows enable everchanging sun and shadow to play on the concrete surfaces throughout the day. But even more powerful is the Church of the Light. Here a simple, cross-shaped incision in the wall lets in just enough light to turn a secular space into a sacred one.

The poetry of Ando's concrete construction makes a deep impression. Its bold expression could be confused with Brutalism. However, this approach is not Ando's point of origin nor that of most Japanese architects who work with the material. Simply put, not every concrete building can be called Brutalist. On the contrary, Ando's architecture inside and out is homegrown. In terms of materiality, craftsmanship and the connection to nature, it is a logical extension of Japan's own traditions.

Pantin Administrative Centre (now the National Centre of Dance)

Jacques Kalisz with Jean Perrottet, 1973

Pantin, France

Yale Center for British Art

Louis Kahn, 1974

New Haven, CT, USA

Dirk Engelen House

Jacky Cuylen, 1975

Antwerp, Belgium

Earl W Brydges Public Library

Paul Rudolph, 1974

Niagara Falls, NY, USA

Holy Family Church

Paolo Portoghesi, Vittorio Gigliotti, 1971–74
Salerno, Italy

Jaú Bus Station

João Batista Vilanova Artigas, 1975
São Paulo, Brazil

Lugdunum Museum

Bernard Zehrfuss, 1972–75
Lyon, France

Roger Stevens Building, University of Leeds

Chamberlin, Powell and Bon, 1963–75

Leeds, United Kingdom

Cosenza Railway Station

S Rossi, C Tropea and M Desideri, 1970–75

Cosenza, Italy

Praxis House

Agustín Hernández Navarro, 1975
Mexico City, Mexico

Our Lady Help of Christians Church

Arrigo Arrighetti, 1976
Milan, Italy

Paulo Chedid Simão House

Ruy Ohtake, 1976

São Paulo, Brazil

A Monumental Metro

Deane Madsen

Washington, DC is filled with grand civic buildings and monuments. What more appropriate approach could there be than to make its transit system likewise monumental? That was the tack taken by Harry Weese & Associates, and it was a remarkably successful one.

In the mid-1950s, planners in Washington began to call for a transit system, ramping up enough support that President Eisenhower established a National Capital Transportation Agency (NCTA) in July 1960; thus began a regional plan calling for a system of 101 miles of rail coverage.

Architect Harry Weese was already in the area, working with IM Pei on the urban renewal of Southwest Washington. Weese was responsible for the Arena Stage (now known as the Fichandler Stage) near the waterfront, to which he would add another theatre in 1971. When a request for proposals arrived in December 1965, he was already familiar with the region and its elegant edifices, from the Capital to Union Station to the White House, and across the monumental core defined by the National Mall.

Quickly submitting a proposal, Weese found resonance with the selection committee through his attention to the appropriate grandeur of the rail system, as well as to its future riders, according to historians Robert Bruegmann and Kathleen Murphy Skolnik: "What impressed the interviewers most about Weese was his interest in the people who would be riding the subway. His concern for comfort, safety and ease of orientation and his vision of dignified urban structures, durable and handsome materials, and open attractive spaces led the NCTA to recommend Harry Weese & Associates as the architect for the system."

Weese and his team—most notably including Stanley Allan, who documented this process in a book of his own—travelled the world to seek out the best elements of each major system, from ticket booths and station-attendant uniforms to railcars and the stations themselves.

Confronted with the mixed topography and geological conditions of the capital city, Weese's team first aimed to carve directly into bedrock for deeper stations (such as Dupont Circle) and to employ a cut-and-cover strategy for the downtown area (i.e. dig down from above, insert station, then cover the hole). In July 1966, Weese was considering an elliptical cross-section with trains at the centre and platforms close to its edges.

Being sited within the capital, the fledgling transit agency (NCTA was later to become WMATA—the Washington Metropolitan Area Transit Authority) was subject to several layers of review and approval. The Commission of Fine Arts (CFA) gave the most formative feedback: on the committee were journalist Aline Saarinen (widow of architect Eero Saarinen) and architect Gordon Bunshaft, the latter of whom had at one point been Weese's boss, which likely contributed to his criticism of Weese's early exposed rock designs.

Quickly, the CFA arrived at the conclusion that, as interesting as station variety might be in other cities, such a strategy would not be right for Washington; building a network from scratch, and with haste, required deployment of a standard approach that could accommodate a variety of station conditions.

Thus Weese and his team came up with a palette of materials: bronze for handrails, escalators and elevators; hexagonal quarry tile in an earthy, reddish brown for the platforms; granite for the platform edges and benches; and for the stations themselves, vaulted concrete, to be illuminated indirectly from below.

Weese arrived at the Metro system's signature vaults in a roundabout way: the scheme was proposed early on, then left behind in favour of other design choices; through several rounds of contentious meetings, the design continued to evolve as the CFA pushed Weese for an appropriately monumental form. At one point in September 1967, CFA records show, Bunshaft grabbed one of Weese's presentation boards and hastily sketched an elliptical vault not unlike that which Weese had initially presented. The CFA, thinking they had pushed Weese to this design, quickly approved it; Weese, having circled around to the idea with which he'd started, quickly moved to refine it.

Recalling both the inside of the Pantheon and that of DC's existing rail hub—Daniel Burnham's 1907 Union Station—DC Metro's original underground stations employ coffered concrete vaults in straight runs of 600 feet, to house trains of up to eight seventy-five-foot-long railcars, spanning roughly fifty feet and standing between twenty-five and thirty-feet tall, depending on site conditions. These vaults are structural, bearing the ground above them, but efficiently so, with the voided coffers reducing the weight and allowing for poured-in-place execution. The coffers also accommodate acoustic panels to reduce station noise reverberation.

For aboveground stations, Weese designed a gull-wing structure of central columns supporting concrete arches cantilevered over tracks on both sides of the platform, with a lightness evocative of birds in flight. Formally, they recalled the curvilinear vaults at underground stations.

Weese brought in lighting designer William Lam to consult on washing the vaults in even, indirect illumination. Massimo Vignelli designed the system's wayfinding and signage, with station names printed vertically in Helvetica medium lettering upon nine-foot-tall, dark brown porcelain-enameled steel pylons, embedded with lighting and HVAC systems.

On opening day, on the 27th of March 1976, the system brought some 50,000 riders through five stations across 4.6 miles of track. Weese's initial design persists in thirty-two of WMATA's ninety-eight stations. Following the initial wave of construction, the design parameters loosened to allow for another nine station typologies: underground, stations began incorporating precast panels with larger (but fewer) coffers; aboveground, canopies became more economical, first with flat-roofed concrete and later resorting to painted steel. With the system growing over the last decade to route more than 300,000 daily passengers across 128 miles, WMATA introduced yet another station typology for its Silver Line expansion. The Silver Line stations retain the barrel vault form of Weese's

designs, now rendered in triangulated metal panels with embedded glass skylights in a gambrel roof elevated above the platforms and rails.

Despite Weese's best efforts at presenting a standard station design, WMATA has over the years abandoned consistency; a new station at Dulles International Airport loosely mimics Eero Saarinen's dramatic terminal building there, while another just south of National Airport has a unique format involving pedestrian bridges and a full-length steel-and-glass canopy. Yet many of the original design elements—hexagonal tiles, now etched into grittier precast sections to reduce slippage; Vignelli's Helvetica-type treatment; granite platform edges—persist. As the Metro system approaches its fiftieth birthday, Weese's "precise, immaculate and colossal" strategy has been praised as "the largest single public works project in history", and described as "one of the few new places in Washington that has true grandeur architecturally". Having expanded far beyond Weese's earliest imaginings, the Metro truly is monumental.

L'Enfant Plaza
All Trains
L'Enfant Plaza
L'Enfant Plaza

L'Enfant Plaza Metro Station

Harry Weese, 1977

Washington, DC, USA

Wotruba Church

Fritz Wotruba, 1976
Vienna, Austria

The College of Mexico

A Zabludovsky, T González de León, 1976
Mexico City, Mexico

Chapel of the Assumption

Laureano Forero, Rodrigo Arboleda Halaby, 1976
Medellín, Colombia

Complexe Desjardins

Société La Haye-Ouellet;
Longpré, Marchand, Goudreau;
Blouin et Blouin; Gauthier, Guité, Roy;
Ouellet et Reeves, 1976
Montréal, QC, Canada

RW&CO
EN METTRE PLEIN

PRÉFONTAINE

Préfontaine Métro Station
Henri Brillon, 1976
Montréal, QC, Canada

Westin Bonaventure Hotel

John Portman, 1974–77

Los Angeles, CA, USA

Church of Saint Bartholomew

Francesco Vacchini, 1972–78

Treviso, Italy

Eglinton West Station

Arthur Erickson, 1978
Toronto, ON, Canada

Villa Ottolenghi

Carlo Scarpa, 1974–78

Bardolino, Italy

Sava Centre: Architecture of Soft Power

Ljubica Slavković

The Sava Centre is where Socialist Yugoslavia embraced the world—and, some say, where it came to an end. Located on the Sava River's left bank in Novi Beograd (New Belgrade), which was the representative capital in the making, the building played a critical role in twentieth-century geopolitics. In its early years alone, it hosted the Non-Aligned Movement leaders, the IMF, the World Bank and the League of Communists. It was where Miles Davis and the Bolshoi Theatre shared the stage in the midst of the Cold War. It became a place of defining cultural moments, hosting pioneering techno parties, the annual International Film Festival, a TV station that shaped our childhoods, bustling retail stores and more. At the nexus of politics and culture, East and West, the Sava Centre was designed to redraw the map.

Like all iconic architecture, it was built to rebrand and to symbolise. As a founding member of the Non-Aligned Movement, defying the East-West polarisation with its so-called Third Way, Socialist Yugoslavia sought to send a message with the world's most modern congress hall, built under the politics of peace and coexistence. Designed by Stojan Maksimović, this technological marvel, later nominated for the Pritzker Prize, was to be built in less than a year.

In Helsinki in 1975, the lifelong president of Socialist Yugoslavia, Josip Broz Tito, embarked on what would become the diplomatic high point of Yugoslav foreign policy. Belgrade was to host the Conference on Security and Co-operation (CSCE)—later to become the Organisation for Security and Co-operation in Europe (OSCE)—a driving force on vital issues of peace, security and human rights in Europe and Central Asia. It was a bold decision, as Belgrade lacked a venue of such scale and functionality, and time was scarce. The political imperative to join the preceding hosts, the neutral states of Finland and Switzerland, lay in Yugoslavia's opposition to a world divided between two superpowers. It was a collective effort and a statement that self-managing Socialist Yugoslavia could, in Tito's words, "construct everything which is being created in other highly developed countries". It was an act of power, embedded in the architecture of high Modernism.

Forged from raw concrete and vast glass panels intersected by dark steel, the Sava Centre is an imposing structure in cascading forms, appearing to have been shaped by grand tectonic shifts. The unfinished surfaces of its constructive elements emphasise strength and functionality, a representation of raw power. The interior, meanwhile, reveals their decorative potential. Designed by architect Aleksandar Šaletić, it conveys a different kind of strength altogether. There is a sense of intimacy and connection in the deep rubber floors and dark leather sofas, beneath the branches of green pipes and orange ventilation cones, bathed in the play of reflections and the grounded warmth of raw surfaces. In its interior, every element is a powerful emotion. It is here that the Sava Centre displays its true power—a soft one.

The "technical truths" of the twentieth century were embodied in the Sava Centre's structure of bare elements. The prominent pipes in the interior, for example, were inspired by the so-called "urban machine" in the heart of Paris, the Pompidou Centre. Yet the heart of the Sava Centre was far from mechanical. The craftsmanship of design finely tuned its core to human scale and comfort. The unity of architecture, furniture and equipment warmed the coolness of its steel and eased the strict lines of visible installations and concrete constructions.

The interior was fitted to host in comfort. It grew out of the belief that the environment serves as a backdrop where one must never feel like an intruder. In the spirit of the finest diplomacy, the representative architecture was designed not to be spectacular, but to foster security and closeness. The vast, modern and sleek congress and cultural centre was scaled to the human form. Its interior was crafted with one thing in mind: to create a sense of belonging. For the many generations of visitors and countries it belonged to, it provided exactly that.

The interior surface spreads across 100,000 square metres, consisting of enormous foyers, congress and multifunctional halls, small meeting rooms, administrative and business units, free areas, corridors, pedestrian pathways, offices, cafés, restaurants, snack bars, shops, auxiliary rooms and much more.

It was designed to evoke the feeling of a city space, with large passages, swimming pools or covered piazzas. In a building of such great proportions and diverse functions, you might feel lost, but not here.

Here, you step onto the soft rubber floor and immerse yourself in the calmness of its deep blues. The dance of oranges and greens, along with the interplay of the sparkling and the subdued, unfolds around you. As you walk, the city reveals itself. A multicoloured grid of installations and structures downscales the vast space, intersected by pedestrian corridors. On the ground floor, these corridors transform into streets filled with flowing water and rows of flowers. They lead you to squares, places designed for meeting, relaxing, conversing or concentrating. The cosiness of coiled armchairs and the softness of leather embraces you, as the greenery surrounds you. Here, the metal, glass and concrete of the building's architectural core are complemented by materials closer to human touch: leather, wood and textiles. It is a warm, living city that thrives on nature—all within a Brutalist building.

Although the Sava Centre is a place of diverse functions, it was designed around a central purpose: the Congress Hall. This monumental meeting room gives the impression of being carved from a single block, but is actually made up of many elements, from the interior features to the movable equipment. In contrasts, it finds a sense of unity: the jagged metal ceiling and spherical lighting are in harmony with the wood-lined walls and carpeted floors. The most striking feature is the Hall's vibrant floor-to-ceiling textile masterpiece—its soft fibres serving as a reminder of the power of diplomacy.

In fact, the well-judged interactions of man-made and natural materials are visible with every step through the building. Great swathes of raw concrete framed in glass invite a mesmerising play of light and shadow. The majestic halls are enriched with bright colours and bold shapes, while the block of suites designed for delegations fosters a calm and focused working atmosphere. These spaces, looking out upon the surrounding trees and flowers, are furnished with simple, comfortable pieces crafted from red wood, dark leather and white steel.

In the expansive meeting areas, these elements take on entirely different, organic forms. Spherical seating arrangements

contrast with the sharp lines of the restaurant. The warmth of the wood is elevated by the weightlessness of a cloud—a sculptural cluster of thousands of tiny bulbs. The restaurant area is divided into intimate boxes by wooden partitions, which both divide and connect. Even the grand Congress Hall can be transformed into smaller rooms using mobile partition walls. Flexibility is the Sava Centre's hallmark.

The journey culminates in the foyer of the Blue Hall. Fully open to the sky with its slanted, partially glazed ceiling, it is bathed in daylight until evening, when its intricate lighting comes into play. Contrasting the strict interior lines is the softness of the blue-green rug, while visible pipes form a powerful and futuristic decorative element in orange and green. This is one of the many details that make the Sava Centre timeless.

To truly understand the soul of this iconic building, however, we must return to the beginning. An important detail has survived all of these turbulent decades: upon entry, visitors are met with a remarkable graphic map in blue. While an architect might dream of creations as vast as the world depicted here, such dreams are not achieved in outsized proportions, but by considering the small and the soft—the human scale and the connection we all seek. With greatness in mind, this building was designed to place Belgrade and Yugoslavia on the global map—a map that has since changed. However, great architecture is the kind that makes you feel like you belong—and without a doubt, the Sava Centre has succeeded in that, regardless of the era or the country it is in.

Sava Centre

Stojan Maksimović, 1976–79
New Belgrade, Serbia

Belar

Faculty of Philosophy

A Stjepanović, B Janković and
L Jovanović Anđelković, 1974–79
Novi Sad, Serbia

Barbican Conservatory

Chamberlin, Powell and Bon, 1962–84
London, United Kingdom

High Court of Australia

Christopher Kringas, 1973–80
Canberra, Australia

Headquarters of the French Communist Party

Oscar Niemeyer, 1967–80

Paris, France

Pre-Columbian Gold Museum

J Bertheau, J Borbón, E Vargas, 1978–82
San José, Costa Rica

Van Schuylenbergh House

Pieter De Bruyne, 1979–86

Aalst, Belgium

Coati Restaurant

Lina Bo Bardi, 1987
Salvador, Brazil

LIBRE DE SE SENTIR LIBRE

Forum at the Institut Saint-Luc (now Forum Jean Cosse)

J Cosse, B-N De Groof, H Doyen
and W Serneels, 1985–89
Brussels, Belgium

Neobrutalism and the Return of Raw Interiors

Felix Torkar

Brutalism is back. The last two decades have seen a global resurgence of architecture that emphasises raw, exposed materials, sculptural forms and a love for exhibiting structure and tectonics. When it comes to interiors, many new projects take the approaches and aesthetics of the Brutalist ethos even further than its originators. While plenty of projects from the 1950s to 1970s combined eccentric exteriors with rather conventional interiors, many contemporary projects reveal a more-than-skin-deep connection to Brutalist principles of "honesty" in materials and construction. This new generation of architects is not interested, however, in simply retreading the past. Their approaches address current issues in innovative ways and develop strong new voices. Because of the radically different context and time gap, I think it is necessary to understand this as its own phenomenon. I call it Neobrutalism.

Why is this happening now? Multiple conditions led to the resurgence. Our digitalised lives are dominated by intangible virtual spaces, smooth surfaces and ultimately impenetrable complexities. One possible reaction is a longing for emphatically physical, graspable objects and experiences. Furthermore, the broader renaissance of craft manufacturing displays a general predilection to not only understanding how a thing works, but where it comes from and how it was made. Raw, exposed structures and materials reveal all. In the case of board-marked concrete, you can even sense the petrified construction process. Consequently, the aesthetics of Brutalism have become increasingly popular again and have shed the stigma of "ugly architecture", allowing architects to experiment and find willing clients for Neobrutalist designs.

Neobrutalist interiors display a huge variety of strategies and contexts. They can take shape in archaic, radically raw forms like the Shui Cultural Centre in Guizhou (2017), which highlights the dichotomy of concrete as an industrial material that is turned into something inherently organic and man-made during construction. What moved Le Corbusier to coin the term *béton brut* in the late 1940s was to view traces of imperfections not as defects, but as signs of manual labour, to be emphasised and celebrated.

On the other side of the spectrum, the Chapel of Sound (2021) exhibits such intricate layers that it makes you marvel and wonder how it was planned and executed. The ceiling is reminiscent of geological or topographical lines, creating dizzying cave-like spaces. It is a testament to the skill of the Chinese craftsmen responsible for the formwork.

Neobrutalist interiors can also be found in renovation projects that strip down existing structures to their bones. French duo Lacaton & Vassal responded to an impossibly

tight budget to refurbish the Palais de Tokyo (1999–2014) by ripping everything out and leaving the 1930s building in a near ruinous state, highlighting the poetics of its once hidden core structure. Inversely, Buchner Bründler Architekten added a secondary structure to a Swiss mountain hut for their project Casa d'Estate (2008–10) to stabilise what came before. Here, exposed concrete acts as an artificial stone structure that contrasts and complements the surrounding landscape, both natural and human-made.

Another aspect of the Neobrutalist design language is the use of exposed pipes. To properly and honestly reveal the structure of a building, the paths that water, electricity and data take should be demystified and presented in plain sight. While this approach could occasionally be found in Brutalism it has proven increasingly popular in contemporary projects. The patterns of Estúdio Penha are among the most striking examples. In the Casa CS (2019–21), the Brazilian architects take it to an extreme, putting every power line in its own pipe, demonstrating the complexity of modern-day wiring and turning it into a piece of spatial art.

As exciting as many of these designs are, the environmental impact must not be ignored. In speaking to the architects I learned that there are still good reasons to build in concrete and brick. Concrete allows for enclosing huge spaces with little material, saves on cladding and paint, makes maintenance easier and, if maintained well, has the potential of lasting for a very long time, outweighing the embodied energy and resources necessary for construction. Despite all that, the cement industry alone is responsible for about seven percent of global man-made CO_2 emissions and the immense scale of the construction industry even makes suitable sand a rare commodity in some areas.

The continued use of these resource-intensive construction materials therefore needs to be critically reassessed, which leads to the question: are Neobrutalist approaches here to stay, or are we already at the tail end of another wave? If you consider Neobrutalism as literally the use of *béton brut*, its future is uncertain. Considered more broadly, however, as an architecture of raw, exposed materials, highlighting structure, tectonics and low-tech solutions, reducing carbon footprints and invoking a spirit of honesty in construction, it will be topical for a long time to come.

Castelgrande Renovation

Aurelio Galfetti, 1981–91
Bellinzona, Switzerland

GGG House

Alberto Kalach, 1995
Mexico City, Mexico

K ME
NOON

Riverside Tower, Penthouse

Léon Stynen and Paul De Meyer, 1968
Renovation by Glenn Sestig, 2016
Antwerp, Belgium

Tama Art University Library

Toyo Ito & Associates, 2007
Tokyo, Japan

Bruder Klaus Field Chapel

Peter Zumthor, 2007
Mechernich, Germany

Pedro Reyes House

Pedro Reyes, 2015

Mexico City, Mexico

AGUSTIN JIMENEZ
MAKING AFRICA
ITALY

Shui Cultural Centre

West-Line Studio, 2017

Guizhou, China

56 Leonard Street

Herzog & de Meuron, 2017
New York, NY, USA

Punchbowl Mosque

Angelo Candalepas and Associates, 2021
Sydney, Australia

Weishan Chongzheng Academy Bookstore

Trace Architecture Office (TAO), 2023

Weishan, China

Alférez House

Ludwig Godefroy, 2023
Cañada de Alferes, Mexico

Saya Park Art Pavilion

Álvaro Siza and Carlos Castanheira, 2021
Changpyeong-Ri, South Korea

Index

Photography credits

Weishan Chongzheng Academy Bookstore
© Arch Exist

Burroughs Wellcome / Elion-Hitchings Building
© Iwan Baan

CEPT University, School of Architecture
© Iwan Baan

GGG House
© Iwan Baan

Tama Art University Library
© Iwan Baan

Punchbowl Mosque
© Brett Boardman

Clifton Cathedral
© Phil Boorman

Palace of Assembly
© Manuel Bougot; FLC / ADAGP, Paris and DACS, London 2025

Forum at the Institut Saint-Luc
© Ferdinand Choffray

Saya Park Art Pavilion
© Yongjoon Choi

Westin Bonaventure Hotel
© Yongjoon Choi

Barbican Conservatory
© Max Colson

Castelgrande Renovation
© Roberto Conte

Cathedral of Saint Mary of the Assumption
© Roberto Conte

Church of Saint Bartholomew
© Roberto Conte

Church of Saint Paul
© Roberto Conte

Cosenza Railway Station
© Roberto Conte

Habitat 67
© Roberto Conte

Holy Family Church
© Roberto Conte

L'Enfant Plaza Metro Station
© Roberto Conte

Lugdunum Museum
© Roberto Conte

Our Lady Help of Christians Church
© Roberto Conte

Préfontaine Métro Station
© Roberto Conte

Temple of Monte Grisa
© Roberto Conte

Basilica-Cathedral of Our Lady of Altagracia
© Leonardo Finotti

Cafeteria, City University of Caracas
© Leonardo Finotti

Chapel of the Assumption
© Leonardo Finotti

Coati Restaurant
© Leonardo Finotti

College of Mexico
© Leonardo Finotti

Headquarters of the French Communist Party
© Leonardo Finotti; Niemeyer, Oscar / DACS 2025

Pre-Columbian Gold Museum
© Leonardo Finotti

Tomie Ohtake Residence
© Leonardo Finotti

Habitat 67 (balcony)
© Gopnik Family Archives

Pantin Administrative Centre
© Nigel Green

---

56 Leonard Street
© Hufton+Crow

Faculty of Philosophy
© Relja Ivanić

Sava Centre (2)
© Relja Ivanić

Cafeteria, Saarland University
© Marco Kany

Ariosto Martirani House
© Nelson Kon

Butantã Houses (living room)
© Nelson Kon

Jaú Bus Station
© Nelson Kon

Paulo Chedid Simão House
© Nelson Kon

Piraque Industrial Complex
© Nelson Kon

Andrée Bordeaux-Le Pecq House
© Laurent Kronental; special thanks to Chloe Parent for permission

Hauts-de-Seine Prefecture
© Laurent Kronental

Villa Ottolenghi
© Åke E:son Lindman

Gallery Place–Chinatown Metro Station
© Deane Madsen

L'Enfant Plaza Metro Station (essay)
© Deane Madsen

Saint Agnes Church
© Roman März; courtesy of König Galerie

Church of the Light
© Mitsuo Matsuoka

Kidosaki House
© Mitsuo Matsuoka

Koshino House
© Mitsuo Matsuoka

Wotruba Church (3)
© Gili Merin

Palais de Tokyo
© 11h45 / Florent Michel

Holy Cross Church (altar)
© Stefano Perego

Johannes XXIII Church
© Stefano Perego

Resurrection of Christ Parish Church
© Stefano Perego

Saint Nicholas Church
© Stefano Perego

Holy Cross Church (tree)
© Simon Phipps

Roger Stevens Building, University of Leeds
© Simon Phipps

St John's City Hall and Civic Centre
© Photographer unknown; City of St John's Archives CSJA 02-01-058

Alférez House
© Richard Powers

Butantã Houses (shower)
© Richard Powers

Pedro Reyes House
© Richard Powers

Praxis House
© Richard Powers

Chacarita Cemetery
© Javier Agustín Rojas

Former Bank of London
© Javier Agustín Rojas

Salk Institute
© Salk Institute

Earl W Brydges Public Library
© Adam Smith

Complexe Desjardins
© Raphaël Thibodeau

Peel Métro Station
© Raphaël Thibodeau

Thorndike Theatre
© Jo Underhill

Bruder Klaus Field Chapel
© Tim Van de Velde

Kerselare Chapel
© Tim Van de Velde; DACS 2025

Riverside Tower, Penthouse
© Tim Van de Velde

Van Schuylenbergh House
© Tim Van de Velde

Atelier Rosa
© Marco Vedana

Dirk Engelen House
© Jan Verlinde

CBR Building
© J. Verrecht; courtesy of Fosbury & Sons

Shui Cultural Centre (2)
© West-Line Studio

Housden House
© Taran Wilkhu

49th Street Subway Station
© Jason Woods

Breuer Building (2)
© Jason Woods

Eglinton West Station
© Jason Woods

Ontario Science Centre
© Jason Woods

Robarts Library, University of Toronto
© Jason Woods

Saint John's Abbey Church
© Jason Woods

Science & Engineering South, UIC
© Jason Woods

Sheats–Goldstein Residence
© Jason Woods

Yale Center for British Art
© Jason Woods

Commercial Bank of Ghana (2)
© Rixt Woudstra

Great Hall, Kwame Nkrumah University
© Rixt Woudstra

High Court of Australia
© Ben Wrigley

Chapel of Sound
© Zhu Runzi

Author biographies

Blake Gopnik is an art critic and biographer based in New York, where he is a regular contributor to *The New York Times*. He is the author of *Warhol: A Life as Art* (2020) and *The Maverick's Museum: Albert Barnes and His American Dream* (2025).

Ewan Harrison is an architectural historian and a lecturer in Architectural Studies at the University of Manchester. His research focuses on architectural practice and capitalism in post-war Britain and the post-war British African empire. He is the co-author of *Architecture, Empire and Trade: The United Africa Company* (2025).

Deane Madsen, Assoc. AIA, is a Washington, DC–based writer and photographer specialising in architecture. Formerly an associate editor at *Architect Magazine*, he is the author of *Brutalist Washington Map* (2016) and *Concrete Los Angeles Map* (2018).

Gili Merin is an architect, photographer and scholar based in Vienna. Her photographs have been exhibited worldwide and she has published extensively. She is the author of *Analogous Jerusalem* (2025) and *Modern Vienna Map* (2023).

Naomi Pollock, FAIA, is an American architect who writes about architecture and design in Japan. Her recent publications include *The Japanese House Since 1945* (2023), *Japanese Design Since 1945: A Complete Sourcebook* (2020), *Jutaku: Japanese Houses* (2015) and *Concrete Tokyo Map* (2017).

Ljubica Slavković is a Belgrade-based architect, educator and organisational leader. She is the author or a contributor to the following: *In Search of Public Interest: The Scoop of Urbanism* (2022), *Modernist Belgrade Map* (2017), *Bogdan Bogdanovic: Introduction into the Oeuvre* (2015) and *Creating a Concrete Utopia: Architecture of Socialist Yugoslavia 1949–1980* (2018).

Felix Torkar is an architectural historian with a focus on twentieth and twenty-first-century architecture and design. His research centres on Brutalist architecture and its resurgence. He is the author of *Brutalist Berlin Map* (2021) and *Brutalist Berlin* (2025).

Rixt Woudstra is an architectural historian and an assistant professor at the University of Amsterdam, specialising in Modern architecture and colonialism, particularly in West Africa. She is the author of *Modern Amsterdam Map* (2024) and co-author of *Architecture, Empire and Trade: The United Africa Company* (2025).

Mayor Dorothy Wyatt at the
St John's City Hall and Civic Centre
John C Parkin, 1968–70
St John's, NL, Canada